weblinks

You don't need a computer to use this book. But, for readers who do have access to the Internet, the book provides links to recommended websites which offer additional information and resources on the subject.

You will find weblinks boxes like this on some pages of the book.

weblinks

For more information about a specific topic here, go to www.waylinks.co.uk/series/religiontoday/Hinduism

waylinks.co.uk

To help you find the recommended websites easily and quickly, weblinks are provided on our own website, **waylinks.co.uk.** These take you straight to the relevant websites and save you typing in the Internet address yourself.

Internet safety

- Never give out personal details, which include: your name, address, school, telephone number, email address, password and mobile number.
- Do not respond to messages which make you feel uncomfortable – tell an adult.
- Do not arrange to meet in person someone you have met on the Internet.
- Never send your picture or anything else to an online friend without a parent's or teacher's permission.
- If you see anything that worries you, tell an adult.

A note to adults
Internet use by children should be supervised. We recommend that you install filtering software which blocks unsuitable material.

Website content

The weblinks for this book are checked and updated regularly. However, because of the nature of the Internet, the content of a website may change at any time, or a website may close down without notice. While the Publishers regret any inconvenience this may cause readers, they cannot be responsible for the content of any website other than their own.

WAYLAND

Hinduism

Gianna Quaglia

WAYLAND

First published in 2007
by Wayland

This book is based on *21st Century Religions Hinduism* by Rasamandala Das,
originally published by Wayland.

Wayland
338 Euston Road
London NW1 3BH

Wayland Australia
Hachette Children's Books
Level 17/207 Kent Street
Sydney, NSW 2000

Produced for Wayland by Discovery Books
Subject consultant: Rasamandala Das, co-director of ISKCON Educational Services

Maps and artwork: Peter Bull

British Library Cataloguing Publication Data
Quaglia, Gianna
Hinduism. - (World religions today)
1. Hinduism - Juvenile literature
I. Title
294.5

ISBN 978 07502 5265 2

Printed in China

Wayland is a division of Hachette Children's Books,
an Hachette Livre UK company

The publisher would like to thank the following for permission to reproduce their pictures: Anders Ryman/CORBIS cover; Alamy/Saulius T. Kondrotas 10; The Bhaktivedanta Book Trust International. Copyright 2005. Used with permission 13; Bhaktivedanta Manor 45; CIRCA Photo Library/Bipin J. Mistry 4, John Smith 18, Bipin J. Mistry 23, Bipin J. Mistry 24, John Smith 27, Bipin J. Mistry 29; Corbis/Lindsay Hebberd 32; Eye Ubiquitous 41; Friends of Vrindavan 44; Robert Harding Picture Library A. Tovy 11, A. Tovy 14, J.H.C. Wilson 22, J. Sweeney 30, A. Tovy 34, S. Grandadam 36; Hare Krishna Food for Life 42; Impact Photos 40; ISKCON Educational Services 21, 43; Ann and Bury Peerless 7, 9, 16, 17, 20, 25, 33; Photofusion 39; Rex Pictures Ltd/Jeremy Hunter 31; Topfoto 15, 19, 35, 38; ZUL 28

Contents

Note

Christians number years as either BC ('Before Christ') or AD ('*Anno Domini*' – Latin for '*In the year of our Lord*'). In this book, years are described as either BCE ('Before the Common Era') or CE ('Common Era').

Introduction

Hinduism is perhaps the oldest religion in the world today. It was not founded by one particular person. It has more than one holy book and different Hindus believe different things. Because of this, Hinduism is often called 'a family of religions' or 'a way of life'.

Eternal religion

Hinduism is at least four thousand years old. Many Hindus like to call it *Sanatan Dharma*, which means 'the **eternal** religion'.

The Vedas

People disagree about what Hinduism means. Many Hindus say that Hinduism is a way of life based on the teachings of certain holy books. These are the *Vedas* and books based on the *Vedas*. 'Veda' means 'knowledge' in **Sanskrit** (see page 6). The *Vedas* were passed down from generation to generation and only later were written down.

Many experts think that the first book, the *Rig Veda*, was put together between 1500 and 1000BCE, and was actually written down around 400BCE.

The *Vedas* do not use the words 'Hindu' and 'Hinduism'. They talk about *dharma*, which means 'religious duty'.

▲ *The sign 'Om' is often used as the symbol of Hinduism. It represents the sound of creation. Hindus believe that the world is created and destroyed over and over again.*

This map shows where Hindus live today and places in India that will be mentioned later in this book. ➤

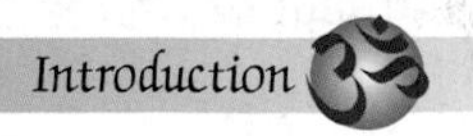

Hindu tradition

Some experts think that Hinduism was brought to India by a group of people, known as Aryans, who invaded India in about 1500BCE. But many Hindus think that the Hindu tradition grew up in India long before that time.

There are three main groups in Hinduism, and each one worships one main **divine** being:

1 *Vaishnavas* – who worship Vishnu

2 *Shaivas* – who worship Shiva

3 *Shaktas* – who worship Shakti

Many Hindus belong to more than one of these groups. They often worship many different gods. However, most Hindus believe in one Supreme God.

Hinduism worldwide

Although Hinduism began in India, there are Hindus all over the world. In the 19th century, many Hindus went to live in Fiji, Mauritius, the Caribbean, and South and East Africa. More Hindus left India in the 1960s and 1970s. There are many other religions in India itself, but over 80 per cent of its people are Hindus.

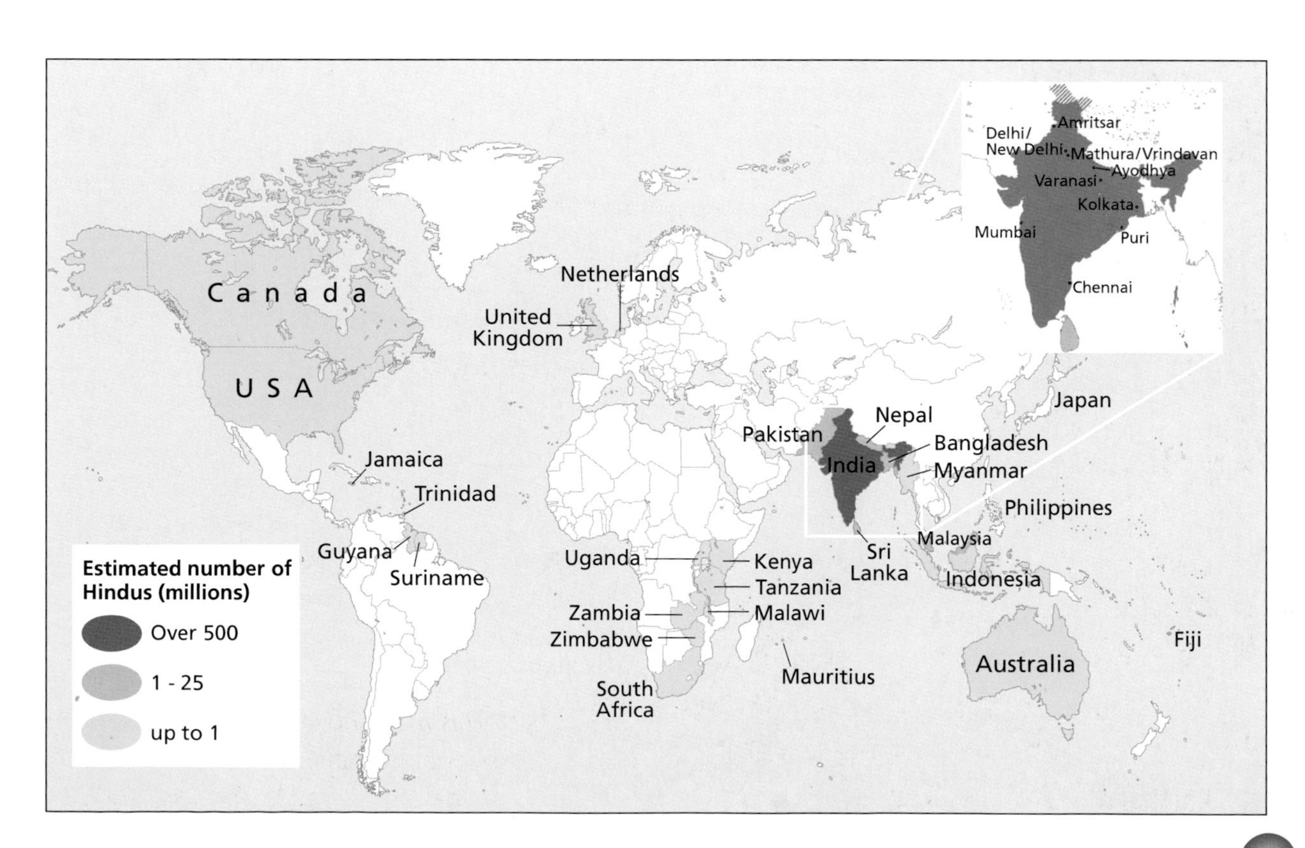

The history of Hinduism

Hinduism's early history is very complicated. It goes back at least four thousand years, and maybe even further. To study Hinduism, it is important to know about its history and understand how Hinduism views the world we live in.

The roots of Hinduism

Many experts believe that Hinduism began outside India. They believe the Aryans conquered the Indus valley (in Pakistan) around 1500BCE. The Aryans worshipped many gods connected with nature, especially Indra, the god of rain. They also used the Sanskrit language. Sanskrit is related to many European languages and it is where Hindi comes from. Hindi is the main language in India today, but Sanskrit is the language that Hindus often pray and study in.

Hindus believe that time is eternal and that it moves in cycles of four ages, a bit like the four seasons. During the first age – called the golden age – people were kind and religious. Today we live in the fourth age – the iron age – where people are cruel and greedy. Hindus believe that real religion is also eternal and is not limited to one time, one country or one group of people.

This drawing shows how the wheel of time rolls along in cycles of four ages. We are now in the age of iron.

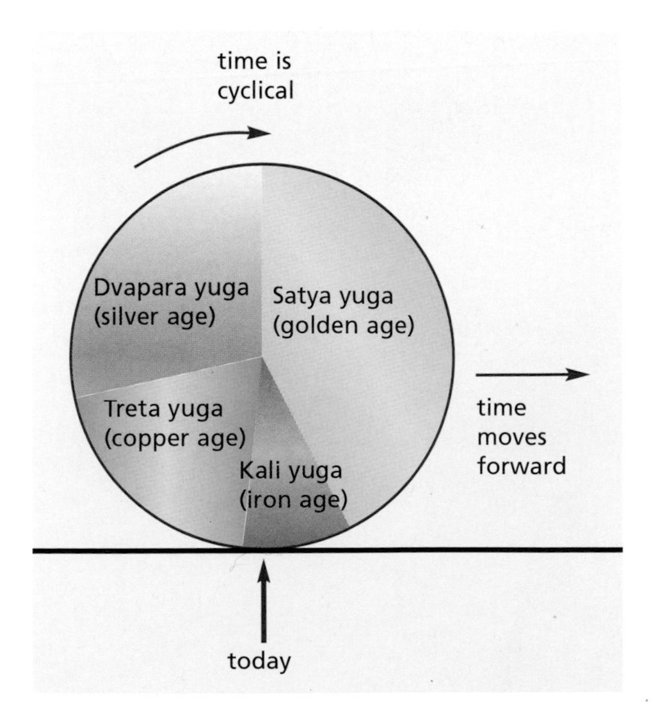

First holy books

The teachings of Hinduism were first passed down by word of mouth. Tradition says that a wise man called Vyasa wrote them on palm leaves about five thousand years ago. Some experts think that the first books, the *Vedas*, were put together later, from about 1000BCE. During this time, the most common religious event was the sacred fire ceremony. It was done in honour of nature gods such as Indra, god of rain, and Agni, god of fire.

Between 500BCE and 500CE, the fire ceremony was replaced by **puja** – the worship of sacred images. The main gods were now Vishnu and Shiva, and the goddess Shakti.

Poets and thinkers

From about 500CE, important thinkers started to shape Hinduism. In the south of India, saints wrote hundreds of religious poems.

Around 800CE, thinkers such as Shankara and Ramanuja started teaching their ideas, which were passed down by *gurus* (teachers). These thinkers had two main ideas:

1 God is everywhere (and is everything)

2 God is also a person

▼ The ancient city of Mohenjo-daro, now in Pakistan. Studying this city has led some experts to believe that northwest India was invaded by the Aryans.

The Mughal Empire

In the 8th century CE, the new religion of **Islam** reached India. It was brought by traders crossing the Arabian Sea and by invading **Muslim** armies. The most powerful Muslim government in India was the Mughal Empire, which ruled India from 1526. The most famous Mughal emperor, Akbar (1542-1605), allowed Hindus to worhip freely. But his great grandson, Aurangzeb, destroyed temples and **persecuted** Hindus.

The British Empire

In 1757 the British defeated the Mughal Empire. At first, the British left Hindus alone. But later, British **missionaries** wanted to **convert** Hindus to Christianity and promote Western values.

While some Hindu thinkers accepted Christian ideas, others argued against them. In 1828, Rama Mohan Roy founded the Brahmo Sabha group, which took some ideas from Christianity and some ideas from other European thinkers. Other groups also tried to modernise Hinduism.

One of the most successful groups was the Ramakrishna mission. It was founded in 1897 by the monk Vivekananda, who named it after his teacher, Ramakrishna. Vivekananda impressed people at the World Parliament of Religions, at Chicago in 1893. He won a standing ovation when he called the audience 'Sisters and Brothers of America'. He spoke of his view of religion that included everyone, based on the Hindu idea that every creature has a soul.

The bhakti saints

During the Mughal Empire, many Hindus became upset with the ***caste system****, which divided society into four social classes. Every person was born into one of these classes. Members of the highest caste were* ***brahmins****. The caste system didn't allow Hindus born in lower class families to get important jobs.*

Leaders rose from amongst the people. These leaders are known as bhakti saints. They spoke of the spiritual equality of everyone. They expressed their religious feelings through song, music and poetry.

A poem by Mirabai

'We do not get a human life
Simply by asking.
Birth as a human
Is the reward for good deeds
In former births.
Life waxes and wanes imperceptibly,
And stays not long.
The leaf that has fallen
Returns not to the branch.
Behold the Sea of **Reincarnation**
With its swift, irresistible tide!
O Krishna, O pilot of my soul,
Swiftly conduct my ship to the other shore.
Mira, the servant of Krishna, declares,
"Life lasts for but a few days only."'

Mirabai was one of the main bhakti saints, and her poems are still popular today.

weblinks

To find out more about Vivekananda and his teachings on Hinduism, go to www.waylinks.co.uk/series/religiontoday/Hinduism

A statue of Vivekananda. His ideas were influenced by the West. Other thinkers of the time wanted to encourage a different type of Hinduism. They wanted to free India from British rule.

Independent India

In 1947 India became independent and was divided into two separate countries – Pakistan and India. Large numbers of Muslims headed for Pakistan, which was mainly a Muslim country. Many Hindus and **Sikhs** headed in the opposite direction, to India. There were fights between the groups when they met on the way.

Hinduism goes global

In the 1960s many Hindus left India, and moved to countries such as Britain and the USA. Many Hindu gurus (religious teachers) also travelled to the West. At this time, Hindu groups became popular throughout the world, and even attracted the attention of the pop band, The Beatles.

One of the most famous groups at the time was the Hare Krishna movement, in which men shaved their heads and wore traditional yellow-coloured robes.

▼ Members of the Hare Krishna Movement in the USA. Its members became famous all over the world for chanting and dancing in the streets.

Hinduism today

After the 1960s, Hindu communities grew in North America, Britain, South Africa and Australia. They built expensive and grand temples.

But in India, trouble between Hindus, Sikhs and Muslims got worse. Hindus and Sikhs had once lived peacefully together. Then in 1984 government troops attacked an important Sikh temple. It was said that the Prime Minister of India, Indira Gandhi, was **assassinated** by her Sikh bodyguards.

There was violence between Hindus and Muslims too. In the late 1990s, Hindus were angry when a Muslim **mosque** was built at Ayodhya (the birthplace of Rama, an important Hindu god). Hindus also became upset at missionaries who tried to convert them to other religions.

Despite these problems, today Hinduism is popular in many countries. It is now a world religion.

The Swami Narayana Temple in London was opened in 1995. It is built of marble in a traditional Indian style of architecture.

What Hindus believe

Hindus do not think that everyone has to believe the same thing. But there are some things that almost all Hindus believe. These beliefs include the soul, reincarnation and karma. Although Hindus believe in God, there are many different opinions about who or what God is.

Atman – the eternal soul

Hindus believe that the soul, or *atman*, is eternal and made of spirit. Our minds and bodies are made of matter.

Our bodies are always changing, but we (our souls) remain the same all our lives. In one holy book, the Lord Krishna, one of the main Hindu gods, compares the body to a vehicle and the soul to the driver. He also compares the body to clothes which wear out and need replacing.

Spirit and matter

Spirit	**Matter**
Never-changing	*Changing*
Eternal	*Temporary*
Conscious	*Unconscious*

'Those who are seers of the truth have concluded that matter (the body) is always changing and that spirit (the real self) never changes.'

(Bhagavad Gita 2.16)

Reincarnation

Hindus believe that we (the soul) leave the body when we die. The soul then enters a new body. This can be a human body or a plant or animal. The soul may even rise up to the planets.

Hindus believe that all living things have a soul. This is why Hindus value non-violence and vegetarianism.

The law of karma

Hindus believe that our next birth depends on our **karma**. Karma means 'action', but it also means 'the results of our actions'. So kind actions bring 'good karma', and cruel acts bring 'bad karma'.

The soul only creates karma when it is in a human body. Animals cannot make choices, because they live by instinct. The souls who rise up to the heavenly planets return to human life after using up their good karma.

Samsara

The cycle of birth and death is called *samsara*. It goes on for a long time, but it is not eternal. The soul can free itself of this cycle. To do this, the soul must become free from all karma and all selfish desires. The soul can then go to God.

This modern painting shows samsara, *the constant cycle of birth and death.*

Dharma

Dharma is often translated as 'religious duty'. The idea is that we have different duties according to who we are. There are two types of dharma:

1 The relationship between the soul and God

2 Duties that depend on which of the four classes and the four stages of life we belong to.

A colourful sadhu (holy man). These holy men have no possessions and live on gifts and donations.

The system of four classes is the idea behind the 'caste system' (see page 37).

One goal, many paths

The aim of these duties is to free the soul from the cycle of life and death. There are four main ways of achieving this, known as **yogas**:

1 Selfless work
2 Knowledge and wisdom
3 **Meditation**
4 Devotion

Many Hindus try to follow one or more of these paths. Most believe that members of other religions also follow these paths in their own ways.

Four classes of people

Shudra – craftsperson, worker
Vaishya – farmer, trader, business
Kshatriya – police, army, government
Brahmin – priest, teacher, thinker

Four stages of life

Brahmachari Ashrama – student life
Grihastha Ashrama – householder life
Vanaprashta Ashrama – retired life
*Sannyasa Ashrama – **renounced** life*

God

Hindu teachings tell us that God can be found in three places:

1 Everywhere. God is aware of everything. The soul is a part of God.

2 Within the heart of all living beings.

3 Outside – far beyond this world. God lives in the eternal, spiritual world.

Other forms of God

Although there is one God, he has many forms. These forms are the thousands of Hindu gods and goddesses. There are three main gods: Brahma the creator, Vishnu the maintainer and Shiva the destroyer. Some Hindus say that these gods are all equal. Others say that one is Supreme, while the others are less important and less powerful.

weblinks

To find out more about Hindu gods, go to www.waylinks.co.uk/series/religiontoday/Hinduism

➤ *Shiva the destroyer. His followers, called Shaivas, think Shiva is Supreme. In this painting you can also see Brahma and Vishnu (in the top left-hand corner). At the bottom left is Shiva's wife, Shakti. Also shown is Ganesh, one of Shiva and Shakti's two sons, with his elephant head.*

Goddesses

The three main gods each have a wife. Sarasvati, the goddess of learning and the arts, is the wife of Brahma. Lakshmi, goddess of wealth and fortune, is Vishnu's wife. Shakti, Mother Nature, is Shiva's wife.

Worshippers of Shakti (also known as Parvati) make up one of the three main groups in Hinduism (see page 5), called Shaktas. Many Shaktas worship other goddesses too.

In our own words

"I am proud of my tradition for two reasons. First, it helps me feel close to God. Secondly, it is respectful to other religions. After all, there is one God for all of us!"

Sunil, aged 22, Oxford, UK

▼ *Goddess Sarasvati is shown here with her husband Brahma, the creator. Brahma is worshipped only in Pushkar, India, though he is honoured by most Hindus.*

Other gods

There are many other gods, including:

- Rama and Krishna, two important forms of Vishnu, the maintainer.
- Hanuman, the monkey-warrior. He is very strong. Hanuman brings help and good fortune.
- Ganesh and Skanda, sons of Shiva and Shakti. Ganesh is famous for his elephant's head. He can remove obstacles, so he is prayed to before any important event. His brother, Skanda, is popular in southern India.
- Surya, the sun god, is especially worshipped during the festival of Pongal in the south of India.

Other gods include Chandra (the moon god), Agni (the fire god), Vayu (the wind god), Yama (the god of death and justice) and Indra (the god of rain and king of the heavens).

➤ *Vishnu, the maintainer, with his wife Lakshmi, goddess of wealth and good fortune. Vishnu's followers are called Vaishnavas, one of the three largest Hindu groups.*

Holy books

Hindus base most of their ideas on holy books. There are two main groups of books called *shruti* and *smriti*. The *shruti* are considered more important, but they are hard to understand. The *smriti* help to explain the *shruti*, often using stories.

The four Vedas

The first holy books were the *Vedas*. There are four *Vedas*. An important part of the *Vedas* are the *Upanishads*.

The *Vedas* and the *Upanishads* are explained in an important book called the V*edanta Sutra*. 'Vedanta' means the 'conclusion of the *Vedas*'. 'Sutra' means a saying that is short, but which has deep meanings.

Main Hindu holy books

Shruti *means 'what is heard' and these books include the* Vedas *and the* Upanishads

Smriti *means 'what is remembered' and these books include the* Vedanta Sutra, *the* Puranas, *the* Ramayana, *the* Mahabharata *and* Bhagavad Gita

The Puranas

The *Puranas* are books of old stories, or myths ('Purana' means 'ancient'). Most of the *Puranas* are about Shiva and his wife Shakti, and about Vishnu, who has many forms. Of the ten main forms of Vishnu, Rama and Krishna are the most important.

People in India listen to a Hindu guru teaching. 'Upanishad' means 'sitting close to'. It refers to the student who sits near the guru, the spiritual teacher. In Hinduism, gurus are important spiritual teachers.

➤ *This 13th-century sculpture from eastern India shows Durga killing the buffalo demon. Women have an important role in Hinduism.*

There are eighteen main *Puranas*. The most famous are the ones about Krishna. Krishna grew up in the village of Vrindavana. As a baby, he was mischievous, stealing butter and feeding it to monkeys. When he grew up, he moved to the city of Dvaraka, and became a powerful king.

Another popular *Purana* tells the story of the goddess Durga. She killed a demon who had the form of a buffalo.

The Ramayana

The *Ramayana* is a Hindu story. It means 'the journey of Rama'. It tells of how Lord Rama, a form of the god Vishnu, searched for his wife Sita. She was kidnapped by the evil Ravana. While looking for his wife, Rama met a group of powerful monkeys and their leader, Hanuman.

Hanuman gathered a monkey army and defeated Ravana. Rama killed Ravana. The heroes then returned home with Sita. It was dark as it was the night of the new moon. The people of the town lit thousands of lamps to light up the way.

Verse from the Ramayana

'If one surrenders unto me sincerely... from that time on I give that person protection. That is my vow.'

Lord Rama to Hanuman

The Mahabharata

The *Mahabharata* is the longest poem in the world. It tells the story of the five Pandava brothers and their hundred cousins, headed by the evil Duryodhana. The eldest of the Pandavas was the heir to the throne of India. Duryodhana tricked him out of his throne and sent the Pandavas into **exile**. When they returned to claim their kingdom, Duryodhana refused to give it up. The Pandavas had no choice but to fight. The two armies gathered in Kurukshetra, north of modern New Delhi. The third Pandava brother, named Arjuna, asked Krishna to be his chariot driver.

The Bhagavad Gita

The *Bhagavad Gita* is a chapter near the end of the *Mahabharata*. Just before the battle, Arjuna looks at the enemy army. Seeing all his cousins, his grandfather and his military teacher on the opposite side, Arjuna becomes very worried. He asks Krishna for his advice.

Krishna praises Arjuna because he is brave and thoughtful. But Krishna then criticizes the prince for thinking that his body is his real self. The entire *Bhagavad Gita* is spent helping Arjuna to understand his eternal, spiritual nature.

After hearing Krishna speak, Arjuna decides to fight. He and his brothers win the battle and go on to rule the Indian Empire.

weblinks

To read versions of the *Bhagavad Gita*, go to www.waylinks.co.uk/series/religiontoday/Hinduism

➤ *Krishna and Arjuna on their chariot. After hearing Krishna's instructions, Arjuna fought for eighteen days until he and his brothers won the battle.*

3 How Hindus worship

Many Hindus consider five practices very important for their spiritual well-being. These five basic practices are doing one's duty (dharma), worship, festivals, pilgrimage and ceremonies that mark the beginning of each stage of life.

Worship

Hindus worship in many ways – even by dancing! The most common practice is puja, in which Hindus worship the image of a god.

▼ *An image of Krishna during temple puja.*

Types of worship

- Yoga and meditation
- Havan – *the sacred fire ceremony*
- Pravachan – *a talk or lecture on the holy books*
- Puja – *worship of a sacred image*

Puja may include:

- Darshan – *'seeing' God*
- Prasada – *offering and receiving sacred food*
- Arati – *a ceremony in which a lamp is offered*
- Seva – *taking care of the sacred image (such as cleaning the temple)*
- Bhajan and kirtan – *singing and chanting*
- Pradakshina – *walking around the sacred image*

In our own words

"On my altar at home I have a photo of my spiritual teacher. The guru is not God, but because he is dear to God, we offer him worship. We believe that we receive the grace of God by serving and pleasing the people who are dear to him."

Sunil Sharma, 20, Washington DC, USA

Holiness in all living things

Although most Hindus believe in one Supreme God, they worship many divine beings.

Hindus believe that anything connected to God is sacred. For this reason, they worship gurus and family elders. The land where a saint lived or where a god or goddess was born can be worshipped. Many rivers are sacred. Cows are worshipped too. Some Hindus worship holy trees.

People light lamps to perform the Akasa Deep puja, the 'sky lantern' festival, on the sacred River Ganges. Legend says that the Ganges water was touched by the sacred feet of Vishnu.

Puja

Puja is the worship of a sacred image of a god or a goddess. Hindus perform puja at home and in the temple. There is no special day of the week for puja, although many gods have a special day. For example, Shiva is often worshipped on a Monday. The best times for puja are early in the morning and in the evening.

Worship can be done alone. Some traditions have group activities, like singing.

Puja in the temple

The temple is considered to be the home of God, or the gods the temple is dedicated to. These sacred images are served just like great kings or queens. The temple priests bathe them, dress them and offer them food. Puja also involves offering pure water, perfume and flower garlands.

In our own words

"When I was small I had my own shrine in my bedroom, with lots of pictures of Krishna, Rama and everyone. Hanuman was my favourite. All of our food is offered to God. My Mum puts a little of each dish into bowls on a tray. Then she puts the tray on the shrine and prays while ringing a bell. Afterwards, we all say a prayer before eating."

Karuna, aged 12, Bristol, UK

Puja in the home

Practically every Hindu home has a **shrine**. It may simply be a shelf in the kitchen with framed pictures of gods and saints. Worship in the home is similar to what happens in a temple.

▼ *Puja in a home in the UK. It is usually the women who take care of the shrine.*

Visiting the temple

Although most Hindus worship every day at home, they often visit a temple too. When they go in, they take their shoes off. They go to the shrine to see the god. People offer a gift of fruits, uncooked grains or flowers, or they drop a few coins in the donation box. The priest may hand out morsels of *prasad*, food that has been blessed.

The arati ceremony

Arati is a popular ceremony. Standing in front of the shrine, the temple priest offers a lamp to the sacred image. The lamp is then passed around. Each person passes their palm over the flames, and then touches their forehead. The priest also offers incense, water and a flower.

During arati, people may join in singing or chanting and play musical instruments.

weblinks

To find out more about Hindu temples, go to www.waylinks.co.uk/series/religiontoday/Hinduism

◄ Hindu ladies wait for the arati ceremony at a temple in London, UK. There are usually no chairs, except for older people who have difficulty sitting on the floor.

Yoga and meditation

The temple and home shrine are also places for quiet thought and meditation. Hindu teachings say that it is important to be able to control our own minds. Yoga and meditation are ways of controlling our bodies and our minds.

Chanting

Chanting is an important way to meditate. Hindus chant a **mantra**. A mantra is a short prayer, or a string of sacred syllables. A mantra stops people from worrying about things like bills or money. It helps people to think clearly. It may begin with the sacred syllable 'Om'. The practice of chanting mantras quietly, or silently in the mind, is called *japa*. Mantras are also chanted loudly to music. This is called kirtan.

Two mantras

"Om Namah Shivaya"
("I bow down and offer my respects to Lord Shiva").

"Hare Krishna Hare Krishna,
Krishna Krishna Hare Hare,
Hare Rama Hare Rama,
Rama Rama Hare Hare"

("Oh Krishna, Oh Rama, please let me serve you").

➤ *A holy man holds prayer beads during his meditation. He has taken a vow to chant almost 7,000 mantras each day, using the beads to help him count.*

Festivals

In Hinduism there are hundreds of festivals every year. Each region of India has its own festivals.

Some festivals celebrate events in the life of a particular god. Some are also public holidays. Other festivals are connected with the lives of saints.

Festivals are observed by **fasting** and feasting, visiting temples and relatives, wearing new clothes and decorating homes and temples. There is also lots of music, dance and drama, as well as special acts of worship. For example, on Janmashtami (Krishna's birthday) there is a special midnight ceremony.

Twelve important festivals

Name of festival	Time of year	What it celebrates
Makara Sankranti	*January*	***Surya:*** *harvest festival (called Pongal in southern India)*
Sarasvati Puja	*January/February*	***Sarasvati*** *(birthday) and beginning of spring*
Maha Shiva Ratri	*February/March*	***Shiva***
Holi	*March*	***Vishnu*** *and spring festival*
Rama Navami	*March/April*	***Rama*** *(birthday)*
Hanuman Jayanti	*April*	***Hanuman*** *(birthday)*
Guru Puja	*July*	***Sage Vyasa*** *and one's own guru*
Raksha Bandana	*August*	*Brothers and sisters*
Janmashtami	*August/September*	***Krishna*** *(birthday)*
Ganesh Chaturthi	*August/September*	***Ganesh*** *(birthday)*
Nava Ratri	*Sept/October*	***Shakti*** *(and other goddesses)*
Diwali	*Oct/November*	***Lakshmi*** *(also Rama): for some, the New Year*

The Hindu calendar

According to the Western calendar, Hindu festivals fall on different dates each year. This is because the Hindu months follow the cycles of the moon. They add an extra month every three years. The month is divided into two halves – the light fortnight, as the moon gets bigger, and the dark fortnight, as it gets smaller. Religious events are worked out according to the Hindu calendar.

New Year and Diwali

Hindus celebrate the New Year at different times. For many, it is at Diwali (the Festival of Lights). This festival welcomes Lakshmi, the goddess of prosperity, into the home. It also remembers the return of Rama and Sita (see page 19).

▼ *Diwali celebrations in the UK. Diwali means 'row of lamps'. Hindus decorate homes and temples with thousands of lamps.*

Spring festivals

One of the first festivals of the year is dedicated to Sarasvati, the goddess of learning and the arts. On this day, Hindus wear yellow clothes and children fly kites. Soon after is Maha Shiva Ratri – the great night of Shiva. People fast and stay up all night to worship the *linga*, a stone column representing Shiva.

In our own words

"Yesterday it was Holi. We went to the temple wearing white clothes and threw coloured water all over each other. We got completely covered in it! We did this to remember how Krishna loved playing tricks when he was young."

Dhara Patel, 8 years old, UK

Holi

The spring festival of Holi remembers the story of Prahlad, a saint. Prince Prahlad's father was trying to kill his son. The king asked his sister, Holika, for help. Holika had been given protection from fire by the fire god Agni. She carried Prahlad into the middle of a bonfire. But Vishnu protected the boy and Holika burnt to ashes.

At Holi, Hindus build bonfires. Everyone is allowed to be cheeky, even to teachers and parents! Adults and children have fun throwing coloured powder and water over each other.

◄ Holi celebrations and fun in Pushkar, India. During Holi, Hindus hurl coloured powders and water at each other.

Nava Ratri

Nava Ratri is in autumn. Nava Ratri means 'nine nights'. Hindus meet in the evenings to worship the goddess Shakti. The favourite activities for worship are lively stick dances, with all the women and girls dressed in bright **sarees**.

Shakti is often called 'Devi' (goddess) and 'Mataji' (respected mother). In Bengal, she is worshipped in the form of Durga, who rides on a lion and holds weapons in her ten hands.

▼ *A brother and sister in the USA celebrate the festival of Raksha Bandana. Women tie* rakhis *(bracelets) on the wrists of their brothers and other male relatives – even close family friends. The boys give gifts to their sisters.*

In our own words

"We celebrate Raksha Bandana. I ask Bhagwan (God) to protect Vijay, my brother. I then tie a rakhi*, made of tinsel, on Vijay's wrist. Then he gives me a present and promises to look after me."*

Dipika, aged 10, London, UK

Pilgrimage

Visiting holy places is an important part of Hindu life. Hindus go on **pilgrimages** for many reasons. They go to worship God, a specific god or goddess, or a particular saint, or to perform a religious ceremony.

▼ *A shrine dedicated to Shiva on the banks of the River Ganges in Varanasi.*

Practices

When travelling, Hindus often accept hardships. These hardships can include fasting or going barefoot – which is also a sign of respect for sacred ground. They visit special shrines, where a saint was born or where special events happened. Pilgrims go to see the sacred image, receive holy food and make donations to the shrine, holy people and the poor. They often show respect by walking around the spot, usually in a clockwise direction.

Holy places

Most Hindu holy places are in India. The most famous place, Varanasi, is devoted to Lord Shiva. Here, pilgrims scatter the ashes of their loved ones in the holy River Ganges, believing that this helps free their souls.

weblinks

To find out more about pilgrimage, go to www.waylinks.co.uk/series/religiontoday/Hinduism

The holy towns of Mathura and Vrindavan are connected to Krishna who lived there as a child and youth. On the east coast, the town of Puri is famous for its annual 'festival of the chariots'. The hilltop shrine at Vaishnoo Devi is dedicated to the three main female goddesses – Lakshmi, Sarasvati and Shakti.

Mountains and rivers

The Himalaya mountains are sacred to many Hindus. In and around these mountains, holy men perform **penance**, meditating and suffering the cold. Further south is the famous hill called Govardhana. Pilgrims walk around it while praying. The *Puranas* tell the story of how Krishna lifted the hill to protect the local people from heavy rain.

There are seven major holy rivers in India. Bathing in them is thought to wash away one's sins (bad karma). One of the biggest events is the Kumbha Mela (bathing fair) held in different towns each year.

▼ *Pilgrims bathe in the sacred River Ganges during Kumbha Mela.*

Celebrating stages of life

For Hindus, life is a journey. Hindus believe that even before birth, we (the soul) have existed somewhere else. After death, we either take another body or go to God (see page 12). This world is like a station, with people constantly arriving, meeting each other, then leaving.

For many Hindus, there are four main stages of life – student life, householder life, retired life and renounced life. There are also up to sixteen main ceremonies, which celebrate the end of one period of life and moving on to the next. These ceremonies are called *samskaras*.

Birth ceremonies

Three samskaras take place even before a child is born. The parents pray that the baby grows up into a healthy person and a good citizen.

Then at birth, the *jatakarma* ceremony welcomes the baby into the family. The father places a small amount of ghee (a kind of butter) and honey on the child's tongue and

▼ This boy is about to have his first haircut. The birth and name-giving ceremonies are the fourth and fifth samskaras. They are followed by: 6. the first outing; 7. the first grains; 8. the first haircut; 9. piercing of the ears.

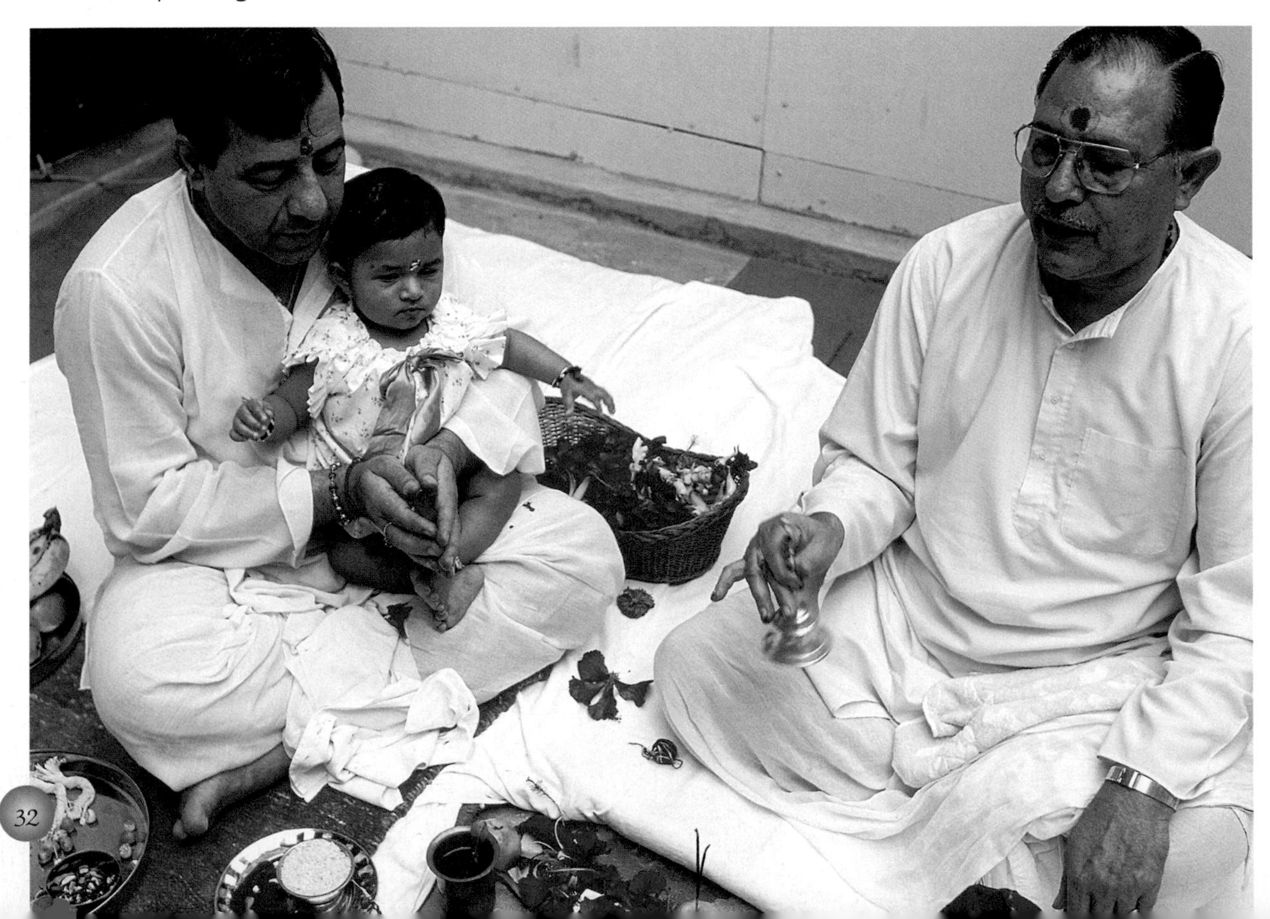

whispers the name of God in the child's ear. Soon after, there is a name-giving ceremony. At this time, the priest makes a **horoscope** for the child and predicts the future.

The Gayatri mantra

'We concentrate our minds on the most radiant light of the Sun god, who sustains the earth, the heavens and all that lies in between. May he guide our thoughts.'

Initiation ceremony

The next big ceremony occurs between the ages of eight and twelve. A boy is given a sacred thread and sometimes a new, spiritual name. He can begin chanting the Gayatri mantra (see box). This samskara represents a spiritual birth and traditionally the boy accepts a guru (teacher). In the old days, boys would go to live with their teacher and attend his school.

Some Hindu groups perform the same ceremony for girls, but girls don't usually wear the sacred thread.

➤ *A boy in India at his sacred thread ceremony. The thread is draped over the left shoulder and falls diagonally across the body.*

Weddings

Marriage, the fifteenth samskara, is perhaps the most important ceremony in a Hindu's life. Traditionally, parents arranged marriages, making sure that the bride and groom shared similar tastes, interests and backgrounds. Young Hindus usually had some say in the choice of partners. Today, couples may choose for themselves.

There are often several ceremonies leading up to the main event. On the day itself, the couple exchange flower garlands, the priest pours water over their joined hands, and their clothes are tied together by a female relative.

A priest performs a ceremony called a *havan*. The couple toss grains, symbolizing wealth, into the fire and then walk round the fire, usually four times. They then take seven steps together. Each step is for a wish, for good food, wealth, health, children and so on. Relatives and friends offer gifts and blessings, and at the end there is a grand feast.

▼ *A marriage ceremony in South India.*

Retirement and renounced life

In the past, when children were grown up and settled, their parents were expected to enter the third stage of life, retired life, often going on pilgrimage. Today, many couples retire, but few officially enter this third stage.

Only a few men begin the fourth stage, renounced life. It means leaving home to become a wandering monk. These men have to teach and preach. The ex-wife of a monk should stay at home and also live a spiritual life.

Funeral rites

Hindus usually **cremate** their dead. They believe that this helps the soul move on. Otherwise, it may hang around as a ghost.

The body is washed and decorated with new clothes and flowers. The eldest son lights the fire and the priest chants prayers, wishing the soul a safe journey. Afterwards, the ashes are scattered in a holy river. This sixteenth samskara is the end of another chapter of life.

▼ A funeral pyre in Nepal, Kathmandu. The ashes will be scattered in the River Baghmati.

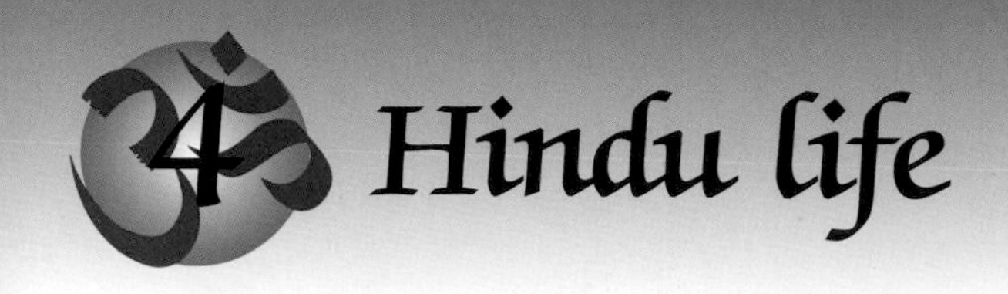

4 Hindu life

Hinduism is not just a religion but a whole way of life. Until recently, Hindu music, dance and drama all came from religious stories. Even the way people dress and the food they cook were connected to religion. The oldest Hindu holy books divide Hindus into four classes, called varnas. Holy books also describe the different duties people have, based on which of the classes they belong to and which stage of life they are in.

◄ A traditional dance-drama in Bali, Indonesia tells the famous story of Rama and Sita. Hindu culture has many tales about wise saints, chivalrous kings, beautiful princesses and wicked demons. These tales teach about human virtues such as honesty, wisdom, courage, conquering evil and protecting the innocent.

➤ *This diagram, based on the holy book the* Rig Veda, *shows how each class is related to a part of 'the social body'. The four classes are: 1. Priests and teachers 2. Government, army and police 3. Business people, traders and farmers 4. Craftspeople, artists and workers.*

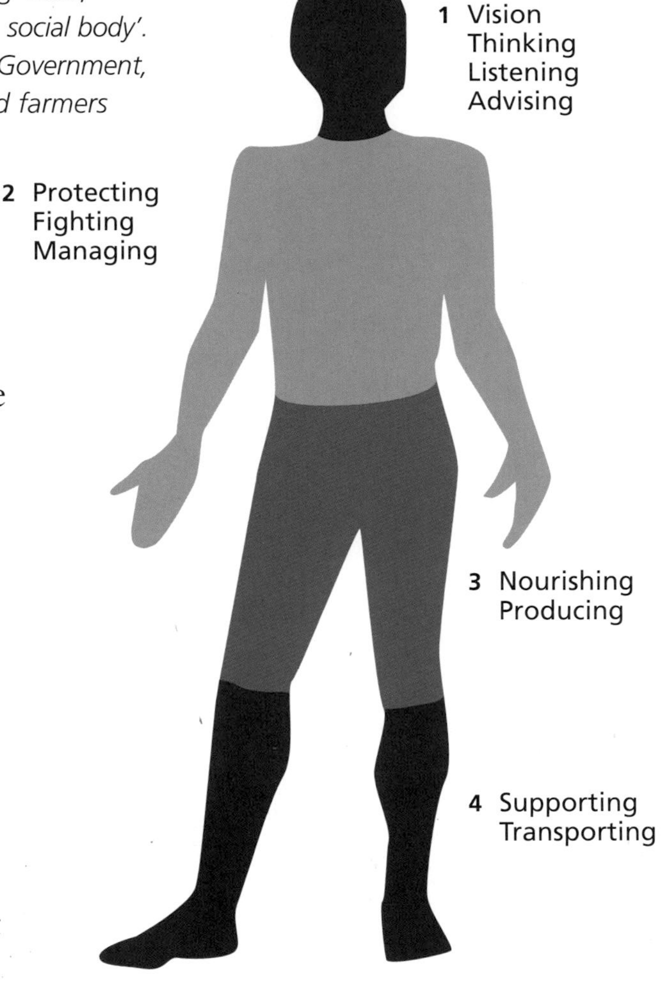

The four classes, or varnas

According to the holy book the *Bhagavad Gita*, people belong to the class that suits them best. The four classes are like different parts of the body. Each part of the human body is important, and works together with the others. Many Hindus think that in the old days, people were allowed to move between classes.

The caste system

Over the centuries, Hindu society changed. Some people of the highest class, the brahmins, wanted to keep their high positions. They said that a person cannot move from the class they were born in.

This is what is known as the caste system. There are also thousands of groups called *jati*. A jati often describes the exact job a person does, a bit like English last names once did, such as 'Taylor' (tailor) and 'Smith' (blacksmith). Hindus are often expected to marry someone from the same class or jati.

In our own words

"My father doesn't mind if I get married to someone outside our community. He's religious but also very open-minded. I think that the caste system is a problem in Hinduism."

Jayesh Sharma, aged 23, Leicester, UK

Mahatma Gandhi is famous for teaching about non-violence.

Gautama's disciple

A young boy asked the teacher Gautama Muni if he could become his student. Traditionally only upper class 'brahmins' could have such training.

Gautama asked, "Who is your father?" "That I do not know," the boy replied. "So, please ask your mother." The boy returned to Gautama Muni and told him that his mother didn't know either. Gautama Muni said, "Yes, you are a brahmin. I accept you because you are honest."

Mahatma Gandhi

Mahatma Gandhi (1869-1947) was a famous holy man and politician. He helped to free his country from British rule. He was assassinated in 1947.

Gandhi followed Hindu teachings, but he did not agree with the caste system. During his lifetime, some Hindus were called 'untouchables'. This meant that they were even lower than the lowest class. They were given only jobs such as cleaning the streets or working with leather. Often they could not eat with other people, enter temples or draw water from village wells. Gandhi renamed the untouchables 'the children of God', to show the idea that everyone is equally important.

The four stages of life

Not all Hindus follow the four traditional stages of life – student life, householder life, retired life and renounced life. But Hindus believe in structuring their lives in this way, starting with spiritual education, then enjoying life and then retiring from society in old age.

Family life

Family life is very important to Hindus. Hindu society is based on the extended family, where three or four generations live together, or near to each other. Great respect was traditionally given to family elders. The centre of practically every Hindu home is the shrine. Hindu families believe their relationship with God should be at the centre of the family.

Women in Hinduism

Traditionally, men and women had different roles. A woman's main role was as a housewife, while a man had to work and earn money. Today these roles have changed, and many Hindu women now have careers.

Sometimes women are treated badly in India. Some families try to make money unfairly from the dowry system. A dowry is money given to a bride by her family. The bride then gives her dowry to her husband's family. But Hindu holy books say that anyone who hurts women will lose all good karma and suffer.

Caring for others

Hindu holy books teach that a good government looks after five groups in society: women, children, animals, holy people and the elderly. So when Hindu people retire, their children usually look after them. In the home, children are taught to respect visiting gurus (teachers) and other holy people.

➤ *A Hindu family in the UK enjoys a picnic. Taking care of children has been the main focus of family life.*

Sacred food

Food is very important to Hindus. Offering food to God is an important part of temple worship. At home some families eat only after the meal has been offered on the family shrine. It then becomes holy food, which, Hindus believe, purifies the body, mind and soul.

Most Hindus believe in non-violence and so are vegetarian. If they do eat meat, they almost always avoid beef, out of respect for the cow and bull. In India, meat is often eaten only after it is sacrificed to the goddess Kali.

Hospitality

A popular Hindu proverb says, 'the unexpected guest should be treated like a God'. A Hindu should welcome a guest with at least three things – a place to sit, pleasant words and refreshments. Hindu holy books say that even an enemy should be treated this way! Hospitality and **humility** are two important values.

Food is offered at a shrine in a UK temple during Diwali (see page 27).

▲ *A performance of* Kathakali, *a mixture of dance and drama from the south Indian state of Kerala. The colourful facemasks show characters from Hindu holy books.*

Hindu arts

Until recently, almost all Indian music, dance and drama had religious themes. The first dances were staged in temples. On festival days, stories from holy books are still acted on stage.

In temples, there are posters of the many saints and gods. But Hindu culture is most famous for its architecture. Temples in southern India are known for their great gateways, decorated with hundreds of statues of gods and goddesses.

Village life

Hinduism developed mostly in the Indian countryside. Gandhi believed that the key to India's wealth and happiness lay in its villages. Hindu holy books say that wealth should be counted as land and animals and not in paper money. Nature gives food, clothes and shelter, and luxuries such as gold, silver and jewels. Wealth comes by God's grace, not through human effort alone.

Religious practices in the countryside are often different from those of people in towns. Local gods are worshipped. The temples are usually smaller than in the cities, and there are many small outdoor shrines.

To Hindus, cows and bulls are very important. Cows provide milk, used to make yoghurt, cream, butter and ghee (a kind of butter). These foods are important for vegetarians. Because cows provide milk, Hindus consider them to be 'mothers' and so sacred. They also represent mother earth. Bulls are still used for farm work and transportation.

▼ *Girls carry their calves in an Indian village near Vrindavan, the sacred town of Lord Krishna. Krishna himself looked after cows.*

Hinduism in today's world

Today, many Hindus live in big cities, such as Mumbai, Kolkata and New Delhi. Many live overseas. Hinduism is an important part of today's mixed societies.

An Indian religion?

Hinduism is changing as Hindu people change. Even the idea of Hinduism as a single religion is quite new! Some Hindus see Hinduism as completely Indian. They are often worried about attempts to convert Hindus to other religions. Other thinkers believe that Hinduism reaches beyond India. It is a spiritual path open to everyone.

Ancient or modern?

It is not always easy for ancient values to continue in a modern world. For many Hindus, caste is an important part of their social and religious life. Other Hindus feel it should be thrown out. Some Hindus would like to see more modern ideas about the roles of men and women.

▼ A modern Hindu temple in the city of Durban, South Africa. Many Hindus believe that the value of spiritual equality, and practices such as yoga, are just as useful in modern South Africa as they were in ancient India.

Towards a healthy planet

Many Hindus are interested in showing how their values can be used in modern life. Indian medicine, known as Ayur Veda, is becoming popular in the West. It teaches the importance of a healthy diet, medicines made from natural herbs and a balanced lifestyle.

Hindus are helping to save the environment. Hindu holy books praise a natural life, planting trees, protecting wildlife and avoiding pollution. Hindu teachings warn against using up natural resources, leaving nothing for the future.

weblinks

To find out more about cow protection, go to www.waylinks.co.uk/series/religiontoday/Hinduism

▼ *School children in Northern India take part in a project that cares for local forests and protects wildlife. Other projects try to protect sacred rivers. Many Hindus believe that traditional values, such as non-violence, can help save the environment.*

The world as one family

Hinduism teaches that many people wrongly believe that the body is the self, and that happiness comes only from satisfying our bodies. People also wrongly judge others by their bodies, seeing them as black or white, male or female, young or old. They will often decide whether someone is a friend or an enemy by how they look. Some people may even judge others as good or bad by what religion they follow.

A Hindu motto says 'the world is one family'. This family includes not only humans, but all other living things. All living things have a soul. Despite the different ways we think of God, he (and she) is the same for all of us. This is the main message of Hinduism.

A prayer for the 21st century

'May there be good fortune throughout the universe, and may all envious persons be pacified... Therefore, let us all engage in the service of the one Supreme Lord!'

Bhagavat Purana, 5.18.9

weblinks

For an overview of Hinduism, go to www.waylinks.co.uk/series/religiontoday/Hinduism

➤ *Hindu priests and an Anglican vicar at a religious meeting in England. Many Hindus believe that all great religious teachers have taught similar truths. Most, if not all, religious teachers have believed in the unity of humanity and of all of God's creation.*

Glossary

assassinate To murder an important person.

brahmin A member of the highest class; a priest, teacher or thinker.

caste system A social system based on four classes (varnas) and other sub-groups; a system that decides what jobs people will do by what class their parents came from.

convert To persuade someone to change their religion.

cremate The act of burning dead bodies until only ash is left.

divine Something that comes from God.

eternal Something that lasts forever.

exile To send someone away from their home or their country.

fasting When someone doesn't eat for religious reasons.

horoscope Working out someone's personality and their future by the position of the stars and planets when they were born.

humility The quality of being humble.

Islam A religion founded in Saudi Arabia in the 7th century CE.

karma 'action'. It also means 'the results of actions'.

mantra A prayer or the repetition of sacred syllables.

meditation The action of concentrating the mind and fixing it on a single point or thought.

missionary A religious person who goes to other countries hoping to convert the people there to his or her own religion.

mosque A temple where Muslims worship.

Muslim A follower of the religion of Islam.

penance Accepting physical suffering in order to make up for something one has done wrong.

persecute To harm someone else on purpose, often because of their nationality or their religion.

pilgrimage A journey to a religious place.

puja Worship, most often of the image of a god or goddess, called a murti.

reincarnation The idea that souls are reborn in new bodies after they die.

renounced Given up. A renounced life means no longer actively participating in the world.

Sanskrit The ancient language of India.

saree The traditional Indian dress worn by women.

shrine A small altar.

Sikh A member of the Sikh religion, founded in the 16th century by Guru Nanak.

yoga 'Union', specifically with God; a kind of exercise that aims at joining the soul with God.

Timeline

c.3000BCE	According to Hindu tradition, Krishna appears on earth and speaks the *Bhagavad Gita* (Song of God)
c.1500BCE	Aryans invade India, bringing the beginnings of Hinduism
c.1500-500BCE	*Vedas* composed in the ancient language of Sanskrit
c.500BCE-500CE	The holy books the *Puranas* and *Ramayana* are written
500-1000CE	Saints in southern India compose many devotional poems
800	Shankara re-establishes importance of the Hindu holy books
c.1050	Ramanuja teaches that God is personal, living beyond this world
1200-1500	Muslims become powerful in the north, but Hindu kings reign in the south of India
1526	Mughal Empire founded in India. Many Bhakti saints live around this time
1600s and 1700s	Many Europeans arrive in India, mainly to trade
1757	India is ruled by Britain
1828	Brahmo Sabha founded, one of many groups that try to modernise Hinduism
1830 onwards	Many Hindus migrate to Fiji, Malaysia, Mauritius, the Caribbean, East Africa and South Africa
1858	India becomes a part of the British Empire
1869	Birth of Mahatma Gandhi
1897	Ramakrishna Mission established in Kolkata
1947	India becomes independent
1950s-1970s	Many Hindus go to live in North America, in the UK and in other countries, such as Holland and Australia
1960s	Indian thought and practices such as yoga become popular in the West, with groups such as Transcendental Meditation and the Hare Krishna Movement
1990 onwards	Hindu communities grow in the West, building many large temples

Further reading

Religions of the World: Hinduism by Sue Penney (Heinemann, 2003)

Introducing Religions: Hinduism by Sue Penney (Heinemann, 2006)

Beliefs and Cultures: Hindu by Anita Ganeri (Franklin Watts, 2004)

Hindu Festivals Through the Year by Anita Ganeri (Franklin Watts, 2003)

Index